CONTENTS

Introduction

Pollution is damage to the world we live in. It affects the air we breathe, the water we drink, the sounds we hear and even the sky we can see at night.

Pollution may harm human health and cause damage to the world around us – the plants and animals and the habitats they live in.

This book explains the causes of pollution and its effects. It looks at ways to control and reduce pollution.

Your Environment

POLLUTION

Cindy Leaney

Franklin Watts
London • Sydney

How to use this book

This series has been developed for group use in the classroom, as well as for students reading on their own. Its differentiated text allows students of mixed reading abilities to enjoy reading and talking about the same topic.

① The main text and ② picture captions give essential information in short, simple sentences. They are set in the © Sassoon font as recommended by the National Literacy Strategy document *Writing in the Early Years*. This font style helps students bridge the gap between their reading and writing skills.

③ Below each picture caption is a subtext that explains the pictures in greater detail, using more complicated sentence structures and vocabulary.

④ Text backgrounds are cream or a soft yellow to reduce the text/background contrast to support students with visual processing difficulties or other special needs.

Introduction

Pollution damages the world we live in. It affects the air we breathe and the water we drink. ①

⬆ **Would you like to swim at this beach?** ②

This beach is covered in litter. It is a sad example of how we are polluting our world. ③

④

PAPERBACK EDITION PRINTED 2007

© Aladdin Books Ltd 2005

Designed and produced by
Aladdin Books Ltd
2&3 Fitzroy Mews
London W1T 6DF

First published in 2005 by
Franklin Watts
338 Euston Road
London NW1 3BH

Franklin Watts Australia
Level 17/207 Kent Street
Sydney NSW 2000

Franklin Watts is a division of
Hachette Children's Books

ISBN 978-0-7496-7762-6

A catalogue record for this book is available from the British Library.

Dewey Classification: 363.73

Picture Research:
Gemma Cooper

Educational Consultant:
Jackie Holderness

Pollution Consultant:
Mary Edwards

Design: Ken Vail Graphic Design

Printed in Malaysia

▷ △ Natural events can add to pollution.

Natural processes like volcanic eruptions and forest fires also contribute to pollution. The air near forest fires turns to thick choking smog. Volcanoes can throw ash, steam and gas miles into the air.

◁ Farmers all over the world need to grow food, but farming sometimes causes pollution, too.

This rice paddy provides valuable food, but it also releases a polluting gas – methane – into the air. The use of pesticides on crops can also cause pollution.

▽ Would you like to swim at this beach?

This beach is badly polluted and covered in litter. Litter is the plastic bottles, paper bags or metal drink cans that we no longer need. Sometimes litter is not put into a rubbish bin, it is thrown on the ground. If it is not picked up, the litter is left to pollute our streets, fields or beaches. It is a sad example of how we are polluting our world.

Air pollution

Every time you turn on the lights, watch TV or play a computer game, you are using electricity.

Electricity has to be made or generated. It largely comes from power stations, fired by fossil fuels such as coal, gas and oil, or by nuclear fuel.

Power stations and vehicles (cars, trucks and buses) are the top two air polluters. Air pollution is also caused by factories.

▷ Coal, burned in power stations, is a fossil fuel.

Coal is one of the largest sources of air pollution in industrialised nations. The burning of fossil fuels such as coal is a major factor in global warming (*see* page 8).

⬅ Oil refineries add to air pollution.

Oil refineries convert crude oil into fuel. During the process, polluting gases are created and released into the air. As the human population grows and there is more demand for fuel, air pollution will increase.

⬇ Burning fuel pollutes the air.

After the Industrial Revolution over a hundred years ago, factories started burning large amounts of coal, causing serious air pollution.

⬆ The exhaust from these cars is polluting the air.

Vehicle exhausts release carbon dioxide (CO_2) into the air. Building cars can also cause pollution.

What does air pollution do?

The atmosphere is the envelope of gases that surrounds the Earth.

Certain gases, like carbon dioxide, trap the Sun's heat and are called greenhouse gases. This warms the Earth in what is called the 'greenhouse effect'. It is what makes life on Earth possible.

Scientists believe that air pollution is raising the levels of greenhouse gases, making the Earth warmer. They call this 'global warming'.

◁ Is this polar bear's home going to melt?

Most scientists believe that global warming causes higher ocean temperatures. Glaciers and ice caps may melt and water levels may rise as a result. In the last 100 years, Earth's temperature has risen just over half a degree Celsius (°C) and the level of the oceans has risen about 15-20cm (6-8 inches).

▷ Long-term weather patterns may change.

Global warming may cause more extreme weather such as hurricanes and floods.

⬇ Air pollution can cause health problems – especially in children and older people.

Vehicles and factories can pollute the air in busy cities. This can cause breathing problems like asthma for the people living there.

⬇ Some places may become too warm or cold, or too dry or too wet, for certain plants and animals to thrive.

Climate change may mean that some crops will not survive in places where they have grown for hundreds of years.

Food chains may be destroyed and those animals and plants that cannot adapt will die out.

What is acid rain?

Chemicals from burning fossil fuels in power stations and vehicle exhausts build up in the atmosphere. They combine with water to form acid rain. Places close to very industrial areas can be badly affected. Acid rain can also be carried great distances.

When acid rain falls on forests and in lakes, it can cause serious damage to local ecosystems. It can harm and kill plants and fish.

The pollutants that cause acid rain can be harmful to humans, causing asthma or bronchitis.

◁ Acid rain damages the leaves and needles of trees.

Damage to leaves, needles and soil from acid rain can cause trees to grow more slowly, or even die.

◁ Chemicals from acid rain can build up in lakes.

Although acid rain can build up in lakes and poison plant life, it is not poisonous for humans.

△ Acid rain from forests may run off into streams and lakes.

Fish – and fish-eating birds and animals – are affected by acid rain when the runoff from forests enters streams and lakes, even when the increase in acidity is very slight.

△ Acid rain damages buildings, statues and monuments like the ancient Acropolis.

Acid rain dissolves stone and corrodes metals. Scientists say that the pollution in the atmosphere has caused more damage to the Acropolis in Athens, Greece in 25 years than natural erosion has caused in the last 25 centuries!

Lakes, rivers and reservoirs

Lakes, rivers and reservoirs can become polluted in various ways.

Chemicals can build up to harmful levels from acid rain. Factories discharge waste into rivers. The runoff from farmers' fields can also pollute.

When fertiliser is washed into a lake, algae will swiftly develop and grow. Having choked the lake, the algae will use up the oxygen in the water. Fish and other life in the lake cannot survive.

▷ Pesticides from farms can be washed into waterways.

Pesticides prevent insects from eating crops. They can be dangerous when they build up in drinking water and the food we eat.

Boating, fishing and water sports also pollute our lakes and rivers.

Oil from small boats and jet skis enters lakes and rivers. When the rivers and lakes become polluted, both plant and animal life suffers.

Lakes and rivers may become too polluted to use for swimming.

Waste from large livestock farms as well as human waste can be leaked or dumped into waterways. This waste can be toxic to humans, plants and animals, and it puts our health and that of wildlife at risk.

Sometimes factories dump chemicals and waste into rivers.

Many factories also use water from rivers in their cooling systems. When this water is returned to the rivers, its temperature can be warmer. This may be too warm for the plants and animals living in the river.

Ocean pollution

The Earth from space looks blue because three-quarters of it is covered in water. Most of that water is in oceans.

The oceans are vital: we use them for travel, transport and food. They also help keep the world temperature steady.

Oil, toxic waste and pollution from boats' engines harm living things in the ocean – and human health.

▷ **Coral reefs are very sensitive to oil pollution.**

Coral reefs cover roughly 620,000 km^2 (240,000 square miles) – an area larger than France! They are home to millions of different types of plants and animals.

▷ **The oil spill from one tanker can damage sea and shore life for miles.**

Oil is a major pollutant of our oceans. Huge oil spills are terrible but account for only five per cent of oil pollution. Used engine oil washed down drains is a much bigger pollutant. The oily run-off from a city of five million people in one year can contain as much oil as a tanker spill.

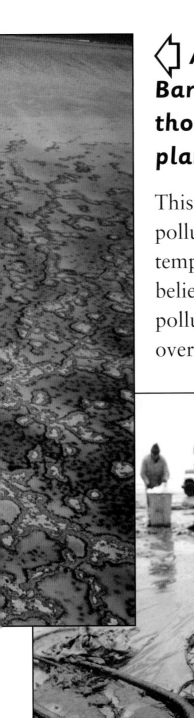

◁ **Australia's Great Barrier Reef is home to thousands of species of plant and animal life.**

This unique reef is at risk from pollution and rising sea temperatures. Many scientists believe it is a result of human pollution, climate change and over-fishing.

▽ **Rubbish dirties the water and kills plants and animals.**

Animals may become tangled up in plastic rubbish, or mistake things like plastic six-pack rings for food. This can block their digestion or cause them to choke. Dangerous toxic waste can also be dumped in the oceans.

What happens to soil?

Clean, healthy soil is important to everyone. Farmers need it to grow crops. Habitats that support animal and plant life rely on healthy soil.

Soil is a mixture of plant, animal and mineral materials. It takes thousands of years for soil to form.

Soil is polluted by waste from towns and cities, farm chemicals, bad irrigation and mining.

△ Bad irrigation can make the soil too salty for crops to grow.

Irrigation on land with poor drainage may cause salt deposits to form. This makes the soil too saline and crops may fail.

⬆ City landfill sites can pollute the soil.

When a landfill site becomes overfilled it may contaminate the soil around it or leak poisonous chemicals into underground water sources.

⬅ Soil is also affected by deforestation – cutting down trees.

When forest areas are cut down and cleared, the thin layer of soil that was there erodes. Rain will wash the soil away, turning it to silt. The silt then clogs waterways, damaging plants and animal life.

⬆ Pesticides can stay in soil for a long time. They are dangerous to birds and other animals.

About 50 years ago, an insecticide called DDT was used by many farmers. Then the insects became resistant to it – it didn't kill them anymore. But the chemical stayed in the soil, passed from plants to wildlife, and then to birds of prey like eagles. The birds' eggshells became weak and broke, and many birds of prey became endangered as a result.

What happens to rubbish?

Waste is rubbish. Solid waste is the metal, paper, wood or plastic that is no longer needed. Liquid waste is oil and chemicals. Industrialised countries produce millions of tonnes of waste every year.

Much waste is buried in landfills. Some is burned creating air pollution.

Hazardous wastes are harmful to people and the environment. They are things like paints, oil and household cleaners.

▷ **Landfills are filling up.**

Landfills are the cheapest way to get rid of waste. But they fill up quickly – and can pollute air, soil and water because they contain waste that is not biodegradable. This means the waste will not rot.

Hazardous waste must be handled with care.

Not so long ago, it was legal to dump hazardous waste in solid waste landfill sites – or even into lakes, rivers and oceans! Now there are laws against this.

Household hazardous wastes like these are common.

We use hazardous products such as paint, household cleaners and weed killer all the time. Their containers do not rot.

Recycling plastic, cardboard, glass and cans makes a difference.

Recycling is an important way to reduce the amount of waste that ends up in landfills. Waste can be sorted at home ready for collection and recycling.

19

Noise pollution

Noise is unpleasant sound. Traffic sounds, airplanes, trains, industry, construction and very loud music all produce noise.

Noise that makes people angry, afraid, or stops them from sleeping is a form of pollution. Noise pollution is a constant problem in cities.

Noise pollution is different from other types of pollution. Once the noise stops, it is gone from the environment – not like the chemicals and other pollutants in air, water, or soil.

▷ **A jet taking off makes a very loud noise.**

The noise from some jets taking off 600 metres (2,000 ft) away makes a noise as loud as a car horn that is only 1 metre (3 feet) away!

This workman is wearing ear protection.

People working with loud machines should wear ear defenders to stop the noise from harming their hearing.

Underwater noise pollution can affect whales.

Whales use sounds to help them navigate the oceans. Noise from offshore oil drilling platforms can confuse migrating whales and make them lose their way.

Noise – or music to your ears?

Some people think the sound of a car or motorbike engine roaring is exciting; others find the same sound annoying. Laws help to control noise levels and the times of day during which certain noise can be produced.

Light pollution

Do you live in the country or in a town? On a clear night, can you see the stars?

You might be able to look towards a town or a city and see a glow above it in the night sky. That's because there are so many lights in our towns.

We do need some light at night – to see where we are going and to be safe. But not all lighting is helpful. This is called light pollution.

◁ **Light pollution can harm wildlife.**

Bright lights can frighten female sea turtles from their usual nesting beaches. The lights can also confuse baby turtles as they make their way to the sea. Wild animals cannot tell the difference between bright lights and the daytime Sun.

It is getting harder to see the stars at night.

In some places, there is so much night lighting that people can't see the stars. It is a beautiful sight which many city-dwellers are unable to enjoy.

Turn the lights down!

Bad lighting can be confusing and dangerous to drivers. It is also a huge waste of energy. We need well-designed lighting that is aimed down at the ground where it is needed.

The sky above this city glows at night.

Lights from this city are ruining the view of the night sky for miles. Many lights are only for decoration.

Cleaner energy

We need energy to light our homes, heat our water, and power our cars. But we also need clean air, water and soil to live.

Power stations that burn fossil fuels are the biggest cause of pollution. Nuclear power stations provide cleaner energy, but are they safe?

Wind, sun and waves will not run out like fossil fuels. They are renewable energy sources.

▷ **You can't build a wind farm just anywhere.**

Wind farms need to be built in places where the weather conditions are right. And they need plenty of space – each machine needs about a hectare (two and a half acres) of land. But the good thing is that once a wind farm is built, farmers can graze cattle or sheep on the land.

⬆ Solar panels collect heat from the Sun.

Solar energy can be turned into heat and electricity. There are some challenges with using solar energy. The Sun doesn't shine all the time or everywhere, and the panels have to be fairly large to make it worthwhile and cost-effective.

⬈ Can we use waves to make electricity?

We could use the energy in waves to make electricity. There are still some problems to work out. It costs a lot and we don't know the effect it will have on marine life.

⬇ London used to be famous for its fog.

London's famous fog was really smog. It was caused when fog mixed with smoke from the coal fires burning in fireplaces and factories all over the city. It's much cleaner now that homes can only burn smokeless fuels.

Clean water

Most of the water on Earth is salt water in oceans, or frozen in glaciers and polar ice caps. Only 1% – a tiny portion – is fresh water that we can use.

We need water for farming and in factories. We use and drink a lot of fresh water every day.

We need clean fresh water to drink. We don't want water that is polluted with chemicals or with germs that can make us ill.

◁ We take clean drinking water for granted – but there are many places where people do not have clean water.

All over the world there are people who do not have clean, healthy water near their homes or farms. They must walk long distances to water and then carry it back home.

◁ The water in this stream is fresh water.

Our fresh water comes from streams, rivers, lakes and underground springs.

▽ Drinking water has to go to a water processing plant before we can use it.

At the processing plant the water is cleaned, filtered and then put into a big closed tank or reservoir where it is disinfected. Then it goes through pipes to our homes.

△ Certain bacteria in water can make it unsafe for us to drink.

Unsafe drinking water is responsible for up to 80% of diseases in developing countries. When there is a major disaster, such as an earthquake, hurricane or tsunami, relief workers must ensure that those affected have access to clean, safe water.

Beating pollution

It is not all bad news in the fight against pollution. We have learned a lot about our environment and how to protect it. People all over the world are now working to cut down on pollution.

New and better ways of making electricity, growing food and using natural resources are being developed.

The car is one of the biggest polluters. Half of the world's oil is used in vehicles. New transport is being developed that uses less fuel.

▷ **New cars like this use half as much fuel.**

Hybrid cars can go much further than other cars on the same amount of fuel. At low speeds in city traffic, they run on electricity and at higher speeds on petrol. There are also hydrogen fuel cell motorbikes. They are cleaner and quieter.

▷ **New products use energy more efficiently, so we don't need as much.**

These light bulbs help the environment because they use much less energy than a traditional light bulb. Reducing the amount of energy we need means a cut in toxic gases from power stations.

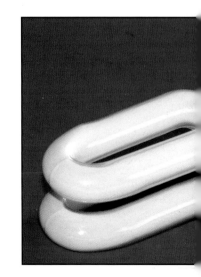

New cars have engines that use less fuel.

Most people are concerned about higher fuel costs. They use cars that are more fuel efficient.

New 'greener' laws help keep this bear's habitat healthy.

Programmes and laws help protect the streams and rivers that support wildlife.

In many places farmers are using fewer chemicals to cut down on the runoff into these streams and lakes.

Petrol Engine

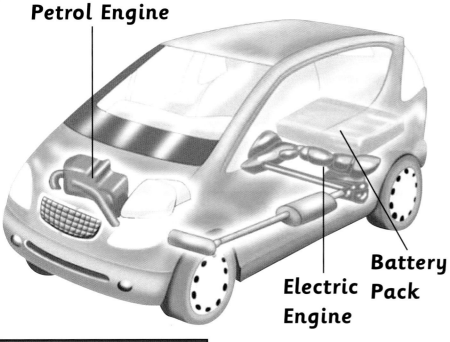

Battery Pack

Electric Engine

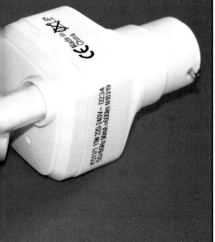

What can I do?

You can do a lot.

Save electricity. Turn it off!

Turn off the lights when you leave a room.

Turn off the TV when you're not watching it.

Turn off the computer when you've finished using it.

Save water and fuel. Cut down!

Don't let the tap run while you're cleaning your teeth.

Take showers instead of baths if possible.

Save fuel – walk or cycle to school.

Reduce your rubbish. Recycle!

Help your family recycle plastic, cans, cardboard, paper and glass.

Recycled materials can be reused to make new things, and we reduce landfill rubbish.

⬆ **Help coral reefs survive!**

You may live a long way from the ocean, but doing good 'green' things at home can make a vast difference to the plants and animals on this beautiful coral reef.

◁ Recycling saves energy!

One recycled drink saves enough to run a TV set for three hours! Each tonne of glass recycled saves 24 litres of fuel. Recycled glass has many uses. It can be used to make new bottles and jars, and even make roads!

⬆ You and your family can make a difference.

Every time you and your family walk, cycle or use public transport, you help save energy.

GLOSSARY

Air pollution – Gases and other things in the air that make it dirty.

Atmosphere – The envelope of air surrounding the Earth.

Ecosystem – All the plants and animals in an area and the way they live together and depend on each other.

Environment – The natural world.

Evaporation – Water or other liquid changing from liquid to gas form.

Fossil fuel – Oil, coal or gas made millions of years ago.

Greenhouse effect – Heat trapped in the air around the Earth.

Greenhouse gas – A gas that traps heat in the Earth's atmosphere.

Landfill – Where waste is buried.

Litter – Waste that is thrown away in the environment.

Natural resource – A valuable material made by nature, like trees, water, air and minerals.

Pollute – To harm the environment by adding unwanted or harmful materials.

Recycle – To collect and separate materials so that they can be reused.

Waste – Materials that are unwanted and thrown away.

INDEX

Photocredits
Abbreviations: l-left, r-right, b-bottom, t-top, c-centre, m-middle
3br, 6br, 6–7tm, 9br, 10–11tm, 11m, 16ml, 16–17bm, 17tr, 18br, 20br, 22–23mr, 24mr, 24–25b, 26–27tm, 29r, 30–31t, 31m – Comstock. 12–13tm, 14mr, 14–15tm, 22–23t – Corbis. 8mr – Corel. 26bl – DAJ Digital Images. 11tr, 20–21br, 21tr, 22bl, 25br – Digital Stock. 2mr, 5br, 4b, 9m, 12–13bm, 26–27bm – Digital Vision. Front Cover tl, c, b, Back Cover tl, tr, 1, 3tr, 3mr, 4–5c, 4–5tr, 6–7tm, 7m, 7br, 8–9b, 10bl, 13m, 13br, 15bl, 15br, 16–17tr, 18–19tr, 18–19mr, 19br, 23tr, 24–25t, 27tr – Photodisc. 20-21t, 28-29t, 28-29b – Select Pictures. 29m – SGA Illustration & Design. 30–31c – Stockbyte.